SCHIRMER PERFORMANCE EDITIONS

TCHAIKOVSKY

THE NUTCRACKER SUITE

Opus 71a

Transcribed for Piano by Stepán Esipoff

Edited by Matthew Edwards
Recorded by Jeffrey Biegel

To access companion recorded performances online, visit:
www.halleonard.com/mylibrary

Enter Code
6542-2063-9764-1160

On the cover:
Illustration inspired by *The Nutcracker* by Tchaikovsky
by Mikhail Belomlinsky
(1998)

ISBN 978-1-4234-5800-5

G. SCHIRMER, *Inc.*

DISTRIBUTED BY

7777 W. BLUEMOUND RD. P.O. BOX 13819 MILWAUKEE, WI 53213

www. musicsalesclassical.com
www.halleonard.com

CONTENTS

The price of this publication includes access to companion recorded performances online, for download or streaming, using the unique code found on the title page. Visit **www.halleonard.com/mylibrary** and enter the access code.

HISTORICAL NOTES

Pyotr Il'yich Tchaikovsky (1840–1893)

Pyotr Il'yich Tchaikovsky was born in 1840. An extremely precocious child who could read three languages by the age of seven, his musical talent was clear enough to his parents that they provided him with instruction on the piano in 1848. However, it was not thought that he would have a career in music, but rather that he would follow his father's footsteps into the Mining Corps. This fate was averted in 1852 by his enrollment into the School of Jurisprudence in St. Petersburg. He completed his work there in 1859, yet during these years he wrote some of his first recorded compositions, including the *Anastasya Waltz* named after his governess.[1] His formal study of music theory began in 1861; the following year he was accepted into the first class of the St. Petersburg Conservatory where he graduated in 1865. During his tenure, he studied composition with Anton Rubinstein and rapidly progressed from an amateur composer to one of great promise.

The years following his graduation are marked by both success and turmoil. The successes include the growing adoration of the public through his symphonic and stage works and his appointment to the faculty of the conservatory. The turmoil included his difficulty in maintaining his personal finances and his disastrous marriage to Antonina Milyukova in 1877. There are several accounts as to why he entered into this relationship, but it is at least clear that he felt in some way coerced (internally or externally) to marry a woman he did not love. They separated after only a few months. Tchaikovsky, already struggling with emotional issues, felt the added stress of this relationship for many years.

Tchaikovsky did not enter the world of ballet until 1876, with the composition of *Swan Lake* for the Moscow Theater. This work, although well-known today, was not an early success, and after several different productions, was removed from the theater's repertoire. In 1888 he was again commissioned to score a ballet: *The Sleeping Beauty*, a favorite fairy tale. The work was very successful, not only for its music, but also for the magical fantasy of its story. In at least these two ways *The Sleeping Beauty* directly contributed to the creation of *The Nutcracker*, and led to its commission by the Imperial Theater in 1890.

PERFORMANCE NOTES

History of *The Nutcracker*

Known around the world, Tchaikovsky's ballet *The Nutcracker* contains some of the most beloved music ever written, embedding itself into the hearts and minds of musicians and non-musicians alike since it's completion in 1892. Yet it is a small miracle that *The Nutcracker* was ever written at all, considering the number of difficulties that surrounded the work and its author.

In 1877, Tchaikovsky received the first installment of a significant annual stipend provided by the wealthy widow Nadezhda von Meck. This allowed him to resign his teaching to compose full-time. Their relationship, while platonic, was very close and grew strong over fourteen years of frequent correspondence. Indeed the income was critical to Tchaikovsky's way of life, but the friendship was of great personal importance to him as well. In 1890 von Meck sent the last annual stipend and abruptly dispatched the relationship with a single letter. Tchaikovsky was quite distraught over this loss, and it seems to be the beginning of trials that would surround *The Nutcracker*.

The next difficulty Tchaikovsky faced was the story itself. He first mentioned *The Nutcracker* (*Casse-Noisette*) literally a few weeks after the premier production of *The Sleeping Beauty* in 1890. With the tremendous success of the latter still fresh, a new ballet was proposed based on the story by E.T.A. Hoffman. However, the original work is quite complex and required extensive work to adapt it for the stage. The task of reducing the story into the libretto is attributed to Ivan Vsevolozhsky, director of the Imperial Theaters in Russia, and Marius Petipa, the famous ballet master and choreographer. Despite their greatest efforts, there was general consent that "the story simply did not lend itself to adaptation for ballet, and that the collaborators came to realize this only after having agreed to produce it."[2] While the original Hoffman story is ten chapters in length with many scenes, the ballet abbreviates the story to two acts with the predominant conflict and resolution occurring in the first. It is in the opening act that

> young Clara becomes infatuated with a toy nutcracker, a present from her godfather Drosselmeyer. She comes down at midnight to visit the nutcracker, and experiences a fantasy in which all the toys come to life in response to an attack by an army of mice. The Nutcracker defeats the Mouse-King with Clara's deft assistance, whereupon they visit his realm, Confiturembourg.[3]

The second act is filled with a variety of dances of nationalistic character, as the Nutcracker with Clara at his side is welcomed home. While the conclusion is both beautiful and full of fantasy, it addresses little in the way of plot or story. Tchaikovsky struggled with this awkward structure, and his concerns with it seem to have slowed his progress considerably. In a letter to Vsevolozhsky he writes "...'Confiturembourg,' 'Casse-Noisette,' ...these images do not gladden, do not excite inspiration, but frighten, horrify, and pursue me, waking and sleeping, mocking me with the thought that I shall not cope with them."[4]

One further burden on Tchaikovsky was the death of his beloved sister Sasha in 1891. In the midst of work on the ballet, Tchaikovsky was invited to tour America. (It was on this trip that he conducted the inaugural concert for the grand opening of Carnegie Hall in New York City.) His brother Modeste had visited him days before his departure, planning to reveal the news that their sister had just passed. However, seeing in Tchaikovsky's face the anticipation of the tour, Modeste could not bring himself to discuss the tragedy and risk the cancellation of the tour. The day prior to his boarding of the ship, Tchaikovsky purchased a newspaper, and reading every word, as was his habit, happened upon his sister's obituary notice. A bitter moment indeed for the composer, and if it were not for the strong persuasion of some close friends, he would have canceled the tour. It would seem then that the mere existence of the work is testament to his skill as a composer, much less the fact that it would prove to be one of his most beloved works.

Preliminary Thoughts

Transforming an orchestral work into a piano work naturally presents a large number of difficulties to the arranger. Transcriptions and arrangements of existing works were quite common, particularly prior to the middle of the twentieth century. Often, concert pianists would create elaborate versions of commonly known works—either orchestral or otherwise—to show the extent of their technique and creativity. Leopold Godowsky created some of the most stunningly difficult works in this genre, but with such extensive changes to the original works that they are referred to as "paraphrases." Works like these were widely accepted and regularly appeared on concert programs of the early twentieth century.

The term "arrangement" or "transcription" best applies to this work, as arranger Stepán Esipoff has made no significant alterations to the original. Clearly, it is an attempt to bring this timeless work to a new audience and extend its performance opportunities through the medium of the piano. G. Schirmer secured the first copyright on the work in 1918.

One must get past the idea of expecting an arrangement to fully and perfectly emulate the orchestral version. It is in most cases simply impossible to include all of the nuances of an original orchestral score; examples of that are present throughout this publication. While it is certainly important to imitate the original where possible, the performer should feel free to embrace the elements of the arrangement that make it uniquely pianistic.

The Piano Transcription

This long standard piano solo transcription probably dates from the late 19th century or early 20th century. (The edition in Schirmer's Library of Musical Classics was released in 1918.)

Little information can be found about Stepán Esipoff. While Tchaikovsky specifically chose a young Sergei Rachmaninoff to transcribe the piano version of *Sleeping Beauty*, Esipoff is a far more obscure figure. As stated by *The Musical Times* in April of 1985, Stepán Esipoff and Anton Streletzi are both pseudonyms of one Arthur Burnand.[5] Apparently, his given British name lacked the exotic sound of his chosen alter egos. A 1902 review found in *The Musical Times and Singing Class Circular* of his compositions states that "Stepán Esipoff's pieces may be warmly recommended to pianists in search of short compositions of moderate difficulty."[6] Descriptions of the individual works found in the reviews include: "an appropriate sentiment of regret," "amorous tenderness," and "romance tinged with somberness."[7] Several of his other works have reviews in magazines like *The Musical Times*. Without these few references, we would know very little about the man who created these arrangements. Yet, while most of his works—and indeed his story—may be gone, he is at least survived by and remembered for his version of one of the best-loved ballet scores of all time. Would that we all were so fortunate.

Fingerings

As in any published edition, fingerings are included here as suggestions only. The ones included here are what I found to work best. Your hand may be larger or smaller than mine, and you should adjust accordingly. However, the choices made were included for more reasons than simply better navigation of passagework. Fingering can affect the color of the tone, the shape of the line, and dynamic level. If at first some suggestions seem a bit unusual, consider that they are likely included for one of these latter reasons. Additionally, you may find some "non-traditional" repeated note fingerings. Typically, these fingerings move from higher-numbered fingers to lower, as in 4-3-2 or 3-2-1. In an isolated situation, this is likely the most natural movement of the hand for repeated figures. However, depending on the surrounding passages, it could actually be more difficult. Some of my repeated fingerings go in the opposite direction, and in other cases, the fingers don't strike consecutively, as in 1-2-4, or 3-2-3. Execute these fingerings with a relaxed hand and wrist, as in a light staccato passage, and they will feel almost as natural as the traditional fingering. Remember that the goal for repeated notes is clarity without accent.

Notes on Performing the Individual Movements

Miniature Overture

The introduction to the suite is full of anticipation, with its generally high register (venturing only briefly down to A2 in this version), dotted-note figures, and pervasive staccato. Great care should be taken not to overburden this work with heavy playing, even in the louder sections. Passagework must be extremely clean and clear to add to the excitement. Repeated notes are a critical part of this work, and the fingerings for these should be considered carefully so as to articulate them distinctly, without unnecessary accents. See the note above on fingerings for more detail.

March

There are few fanfares better known than the opening of this march. This work is the second number in the complete ballet, and is performed as the children are lining up and receiving their gifts. The sixteenth notes that appear in the right hand about half-way through are a clear display of the excited children and their new toys. In the orchestra, this line is performed alternatively by the flute and the violins.

The repeated note triplets in the opening should be played with a forward motion in the hand. Sinking too deeply into the keys will make the repetitions more difficult and unevenly accented.

It seems worth noting that there is one noticeable alteration to the orchestral version in this arrangement. When the main fanfare returns after the sixteenths, there is a terrific ascending scale passage running from the basses through to the violins, an unmistakably characteristic moment from this work. It is missing in this arrangement; including it would perhaps have been physically impossible.

Pay close attention to the *piano subito* markings on the fanfare; doing so helps recreate the orchestral sound as the music changes from full orchestra to brass and winds alone. Some of the other dynamic markings may not be quite what is expected, having heard the orchestral version, but they should be taken as an attempt to fit the work to the qualities of the piano.

Dance of the Sugar-Plum Fairy

The most characteristic sound in this work is the *celeste*, which carries the main theme at m. 5. While impossible to exactly reproduce this sound on the piano, the performer should strive to imitate the bell-like quality of the instrument. Right-hand voicing should be distinctly weighted toward the top notes, with a clean and almost piercing sound. Particularly in the 8va section beginning in m. 37, be sure that the melody rings over the other notes of the chord. In general, of course, care should be taken not to lose the lower notes of the right hand, as they provide critical harmonic contrast to the theme.

For the arpeggios beginning in m. 32, the sound should be warmer in the lower registers and brighten as the notes rise. The strings are pizzicato for the opening presentation of the theme, so a nice crisp staccato is in order for the LH. When the theme returns after the arpeggios, the marking is *a punto d'arco*, instructing the players to use the tip of the bow. This gives a more present sound than pizzicato, but is still far lighter than when using the full bow. As a result, the left hand should be slightly fuller, and the arpeggio sign in the score provides the needed change in the sound. One should be extremely careful about pedaling in this work, as it could easily detract from the character of the left hand.

This arrangement contains one of the most striking differences from the original orchestration. At the conclusion of this dance, most listeners expect to hear the conclusive cadence on the tonic of E minor, as it is in any standard performance of the suite. In the full score of the ballet, however, this dance is the second variation in the closing "Pas de deux." It concludes with a half cadence on the V chord, B major, and then continues on to the next section in E minor. In the full score this makes perfect sense, but in this version, in this order, the ending sounds quite incomplete. Esipoff must have felt that he was being faithful to the score, but those hearing this arrangement for the first time will likely experience a significant surprise. (An alternate ending on tonic has been added as a footnote in the score.)

Russian Dance, "Trepak"

Extremely energetic and in perpetual motion, this work completely embodies the spirit of a wild Russian dance. Great and sudden contrasts of dynamics will give strength to a performance of this work. Be careful that the notes prior to a *subito forte* or *fortissimo* are not accented unnecessarily; stay relaxed through the end of the softer figure without anticipating the weight needed for the *forte* chords.

There is one more noticeable change from the original. When the second theme drops into the basses and lower strings, the rhythmic figure is an eighth, two sixteenths, and two eighths. However, in this arrangement, it is inexplicably changed: the first eighth becomes a dotted eighth, and the two sixteenth notes become one sixteenth. It is even phrased differently, and includes the "pesante" marking.

Arab Dance

Few themes in music are more haunting than this simple tune with a range of about a third. Marius Petipa (who helped adapt the original Hoffman story for the stage) referred to it as "cloying and bewitching music."[8] The LH provides the underlying "carpet" of sound with just enough rhythmic ingenuity to keep it moving forward; try to keep it free of sudden accent. In the RH, the quintuplets should be little more than a murmur, like the mysterious decorative turn of a native instrument. Keep the upper note of the thirds clear, but not so prominent that the color of the lower tone is lost.

Chinese Dance

The original orchestration sheds all of the warmth of the preceding work through the use of the disparate registers of the flute and bassoon accompanied by pizzicato strings. Bright and dark are thrown together, yet they fit surprisingly well. The harmony is extremely simple: a constant pedal tone of B-flat, over which there are only two chords (I and V). Keep the focus on the unusual melodic combinations, paying close attention to the given articulations.

Dance of the Reed-Flutes

Clear voicing is again important here to imitate the high, breathy sound of a flute made of wood or reed. This is a light and bouncing work, but care should be taken not to accent beyond what naturally occurs in the music. For example, in m. 43 the length of the dotted-eighths in the LH is sufficient to keep a subtle accent; take care not to otherwise accent the RH. Additionally, this will help the RH create a longer melodic line. Also in this section, maintain a good contrast between the staccato RH and the legato LH.

The rolled chords and grace notes are a vital part of the character of this work. Don't make the rolls overly dramatic or the grace notes too long. Doing so places too much focus on the ornaments rather than allowing them to contribute to the overall sound of the music.

Waltz of the Flowers

The grandest work in the set, this waltz is an appropriate capstone to the suite. Throughout the piece the tempo should feel somewhat relaxed—downbeats generally steady, but room within the measure for flexibility. At m. 17, the harp's well-known cadenza should be taken with a good degree of freedom, with gentle accents on the beats to create a melodic line. Incidentally, this is taken directly from the harp part in the orchestral score. Consider half-pedaling some in this passage to keep from blurring the sound too much.

In several places it is good to consider the original orchestration to help the interpretation. For example, in m. 45 keep the line very legato, imitating the clarinets. A very deep tone is needed in the melody at m. 134; the orchestration here is for cello and viola. One final example (and many others could be found) is in m. 164 where the flutes are scored with the melody above the strings; keep the octaves in the RH brighter on the top.

In m. 258, there are actually two separate voices, even though the piano score notation may not clearly reflect it.

Watch the LH accents carefully in the section beginning at m. 298. The ones that fall on beat two are particularly interesting, as in m. 300; the fact that it is on an offbeat gives it a metric accent. The absence of an accent in the following measure helps to "suspend" the meter briefly, increasing the anticipation of the next downbeat.

Always consider the overall dynamic and musical structure of this work. The excitement and energy should build throughout, reaching the logical climax on the final chord.

—Matthew Edwards

Notes

1. Wiley, "Tchaikovsky, Pyotr Il'yich," p. 1.
2. Wiley, *Tchaikovsky's Ballets*, p. 197.
3. Wiley, "Tchaikovsky, Pyotr Il'yich," p. 6.
4. Wiley, *Tchaikovsky's Ballets*, p. 196.
5. Nosnikrap, "Pseudonimity," p. 202.
6. Review, p. 817.
7. Ibid.
8. Fisher, "Arabian Coffee," p. 146.

References

Books:

Hanson, Lawrence and Elisabeth. *Tchaikovsky: The Man behind the Music*. New York: Dodd, Mead, & Co., 1966.

Weinstock, Herbert. *Tchaikovsky*. New York: Alfred A. Knopf, 1966.

Wiley, Roland John. *Tchaikovsky's Ballets: Swan Lake, Sleeping Beauty, Nutcracker*. Oxford: Clarendon Press, 1985.

Articles:

Abraham, Gerald. "Tchaikovsky: Some Centennial Reflections," *Music & Letters*, Vol. 21, No. 2 (April 1940), Oxford University Press, pp. 110–119, www.jstor.org

Holloway, Robin. "Tchaikovsky," *The Musical Times*, Vol. 134, No. 1809 (November 1993), Musical Times Publications Ltd., pp. 620–623, www.jstor.org

Fisher, Jennifer. "*Arabian Coffee* in the Land of the Sweets," Dance Journal, Vol. 35/36, No. 2/1 (Winter 2003-Summer 2004) University of Illinois Press on behalf of Congress on Research in Dance, pp. 146–163.

Nosnikrap, A.J. "Pseudonimity," *The Musical Times*, Vol. 126, No. 1706 (April 1985) Musical Times Publications Ltd., pp. 202–203. www.jstor.org

Review: [untitled], *The Musical Times and Singing Class Circular*, Vol. 43, No. 718 (December 1, 1902), Musical Times Publications Ltd., p. 817.

Wiley, Roland John. "On Meaning in 'Nutcracker'," *The Journal of the Society for Dance Research*, Vol. 3, No. 1 (Autumn 1984), Edinburgh University Press, pp. 3–28, www.jstor.org

Wily, Roland John. "Tchaikovsky, Pyotr Il'yich." *Grove Music Online. Oxford Music Online*. www.oxfordmusiconline.com

Acknowledgement

As the editor, I would like to dedicate this edition to my favorite ballerina, my dearest Audrey.

THE NUTCRACKER SUITE

Miniature Overture

Transcribed for piano by
Stepán Esipoff

Pyotr Il'yich Tchaikovsky
Op. 71a

26
mf p p p cresc.

31
mf ten. ten. ten.

36
ten. f ten. cresc. f ten.
8va

41
sfz ten. sfz sfz sfz sfz sfz sfz
dolce cantabile
mp

47
mf p con grazia p
sopra

53 *cresc.* *ten.* *f* *mp*

59 *mf* *p dolce espr.* *mp* *p*

65 *mp* *mf* *ten.* *f*

71 *pp* *8va* *cresc.*

76 *(8va)* *ff* *ten.* *pesante* *ten.* *ten.*

81 ten. 8va

brillante
ten.

f

86 (8va)

ff

pp

92

pp

98

pp

ten. ten.

p

103 ten.

p

108
ten.
p
113
p
mf
p
Ped.
118
p
cresc.
mf
ten.
123
ten.
mf
cresc.
8va
128
(8va)
f
sfz
ten.

134 dolce cantabile

p ten. *p con grazia*

sopra

139 ten. *p* cresc.

144 ten. ten. *f* *mf* *mp* *mf*

149 ten. ten. *p* ten. *p* ten. *mp*

155 ten. *f*

160
pp
cresc.
164
ff
168
ten.
pesante
ten.
ten.
ten.
sempre ff
173
brillante
178
sfz
sfz
Ped. *
Ped. *
Ped. *

March

20
stacc.
f
mf
mf
24
ten.
f
p subito
mf
p
ten.
28
ten.
mf
p
ten.
31
cresc.
f
p
34
ten.
ten.
mf
p
mf
p
ten.
ten.

38
cresc.
f
sfz
stacc. e leggero
41
mf
ten.
mp
44
f
mf
ten.
47
mp
f
p subito
mf
ten.
51
p
ten.
mf
p
ten.

55
cresc.
f
p subito
58
ten.
mf
ten.
p
ten.
mf
p
ten.
62
cresc.
mf
f
sfz
65
mf
mf
stacc.
f
69
stacc.
mf
mf
f

73
ten.
p subito
mf
p
mf
p
ten.
77
cresc.
80
f
p
ten.
mf
ten.
83
p
ten.
mf
p
ten.
86
cresc.
f
sfz
sfz

Dance of the Sugar-Plum Fairy

24
sfz
pp
p
sopra
27
sfz
p
sfz
sopra
sopra
30
quasi arpa
p
sfz
p cresc.
f
ten.
Ped.
33
8va
35

* Alternate ending on tonic. See Performance Notes.

Russian Dance, "Trepak"

(8va)
26
ff mf
cresc.
31
ff
p pesante
cresc.
36
ff
f
42
ff
48
ff
mf
ten.
ff
mf
ten.
ff
ten.
ten.
ten.
ten.

53
mf
ff
ten.
fff
sfz
58
stringendo
poco a poco
cresc.
63
68
cresc.
Prestissimo
73

Arab Dance

Commodo
pp
p
molto espressivo e cantabile
mf
dolcissimo
pp
mf
ten.
p

pp
p
mf

69
ten.
mf
p
f
ten.
mf
ten.
75
dolce
p
f
mf
p
81
mf
ten.
p
p
87
mf
p
92
mp
pp
p
pp
poco a poco
97
p
morendo sin al Fine
ppp

Chinese Dance

17
tr
f
mf
20
22
tr
f
24
mf
27
f
cresc.
30
(cresc.)
ff

Dance of the Reed-Flutes

23
p ten.
p
mp
27
delicato
sempre stacc.
ten.
ten.
mf
31
p
mp
mf
35
p
ten.
ten.
mf
39
p
cresc.
f
ten.
ten.
p
Ped.
* Ped.
*

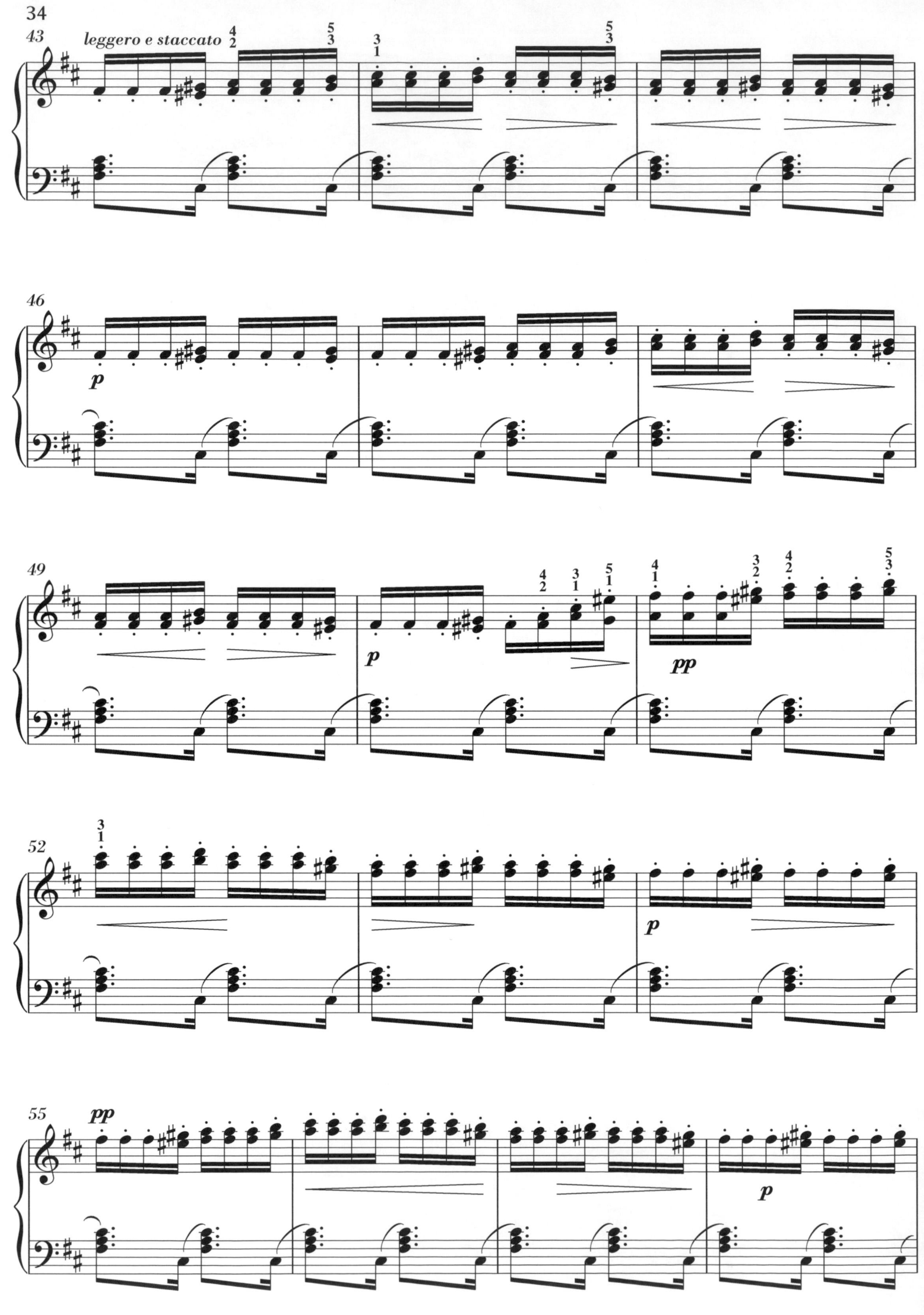
43
leggero e staccato
46
p
49
p
pp
52
p
55
pp
p

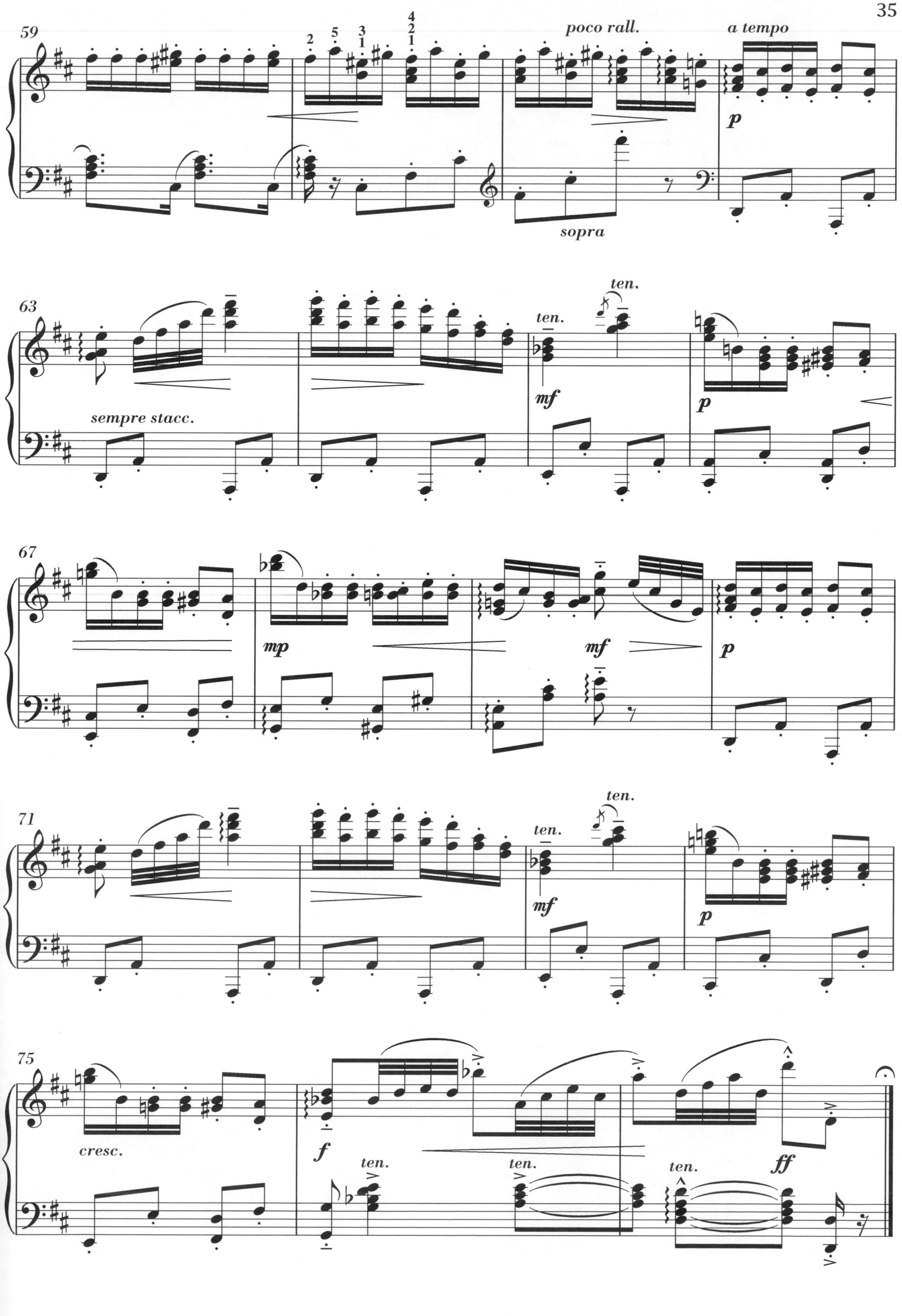

59 poco rall. a tempo

sopra

63 sempre stacc. ten. ten.

67

71 ten. ten.

75 cresc. ten. ten. ten.

Waltz of the Flowers

24 (8va)

cresc.

28 8va

rit.

sfz

ff

12

8va

12

Ped. *

smorzando

mp

Ped. * Ped. * Ped. *

34 a tempo

dolce cantando

pp leggero

p

mp

43

ten.

f

p

cresc.

mf

50

p

58
mp
ten.
f
p
65
mf
f dolce
73
Ped.
81
f
sfz
f cantando
89
Ped.
f

97
1.
2.
sfz
sfz
dolce
cantabile
102
mf
p
mf
ten.
110
f
117
p dolce cantando
125
p
ten.
f
Ped.
*

132
Con anima
f
mf non legato
141
Ped.
148
f
mf
156
ff
8va
p dolce
Ped.
164
(8va)
p
ten.

(8va)
172
mp
cresc.
f
ten.
ten.
ten.
180
ten.
ten.
ten.
3
4
3
ff
pp
poco rall.
ten.
ten.
ten.
ten.
Ped.
186
a tempo
p
mp
ten.
f
p
194
cresc.
mf
201
p
mp
ten.

209
p
mf
215
f dolce
222
ten.
Ped.
229
f
sfz
f cantando
237
f
Ped.

245
f
250
ff
255
ten.
sfz
p subito
stacc.
260
ten.
mp
265
pp
cresc.

ten.
cresc.
sfz
ff
espr.
Ped.
ff
sfz
8va
p sub.
cresc.

296
8va
f
ten.
ten.
ten.
ff
302
8va
ff
308
p
cresc.
f
ten.
ten.
ten.
314
ff sfz brillante
sfz
sfz
sfz accel. e cresc.
320
largamente
rit.
8va
sfz
sfz
fff
ten.
sfz
sfz

ABOUT THE EDITOR

Matthew Edwards

Dr. T. Matthew Edwards is a musician of many facets. As a pianist, he has been hailed by critics for his "...considerable talent...honest musicianship, and a formidable technique." His performances have taken him throughout the United States and to Asia, appearing as recitalist, guest artist, concerto soloist, and collaborative artist. His competition winnings include the Grand Prize in the Stravinsky Awards International Competition, and First Prize in the Music Teachers National Association National Collegiate Finals. He has previously served as part-time faculty at several colleges, including the Peabody Conservatory of Music in Baltimore, and full-time as Assistant Professor of Music at Anne Arundel Community College (AACC) in Maryland. Currently, he is Associate Professor of Music and Director of Keyboard Studies at Missouri Western State University. As a lecturer, he has been featured at the National Conference of the Music Teachers National Association, the World Piano Pedagogy Conference, and at the state conventions of the Maryland, Missouri, and Texas Music Teacher's Association. He also serves on the editorial committee for American Music Teacher magazine. As a composer, he has had major works premiered in Chicago, Salt Lake City, and the Baltimore area, and is a contributing author for the Hal Leonard Student Piano Library. As a conductor and coach, Dr. Edwards has served as the rehearsal pianist/coach for the Annapolis Opera, and musical director for Opera AACC. He lives in Kansas City, Missouri with his wife, Kelly, and their three children, Audrey, Jackson, and Cole.

ABOUT THE RECORDING ARTIST

Jeffrey Biegel

Leonard Bernstein said of pianist Jeffrey Biegel: "He played fantastic Liszt. He is a splendid musician and a brilliant performer." Biegel is one of today's most respected artists and has created a multi-faceted career as a pianist, composer, and arranger. His career has been marked by bold creative achievements. In 1997, he performed Gershwin's *Rhapsody in Blue* with the Boston Pops Orchestra based on the restored, original 1924 solo piano manuscript. He performed the first live internet recitals in New York and Amsterdam in 1997 and 1998. In 1999, he assembled a consortium of over 25 orchestras to celebrate the millennium with a new concerto *(Millennium Fantasy for Piano and Orchestra)* composed for him by Ellen Taaffe Zwilich. Charles Strouse composed *Concerto America* for Biegel, celebrating America and honoring the heroes and events of September 11, 2001. Biegel assembled a global consortium to commission the *Concerto No. 3 for Piano and Orchestra* by Lowell Liebermann with performances in 2006-2008 with consortium orchestras. Biegel also arranged the *Symphonic Fantasies for Piano and Orchestra* based on four of Billy Joel's classical compositions from *Fantasies and Delusions*. These virtuosic transcriptions consist of four solo piano pieces, orchestrated by Phillip Keveren. Biegel recorded Leroy Anderson's *Concerto in* C with Leonard Slatkin conducting the BBC Concert Orchestra for a 2007 Naxos CD.

In addition to his concert activities, Biegel and his son, Craig, co-composed *The World In Our Hands*, reflecting the events of September 11, 2001 with a vision for hope and peace.

PianoDisc has released Biegel's recordings *Rare Gems of the Golden Age*, *Best of David Foster*, *Best of Leroy Anderson*, *Best of Josh Groban* in his solo piano arrangements, and a set of *Classical Carols* arranged by Carolyne M. Taylor. Additionally, he has recorded his solo transcription of the complete *Four Seasons* by Vivaldi, along with Grieg's *Suite in the Antique Style (after Holberg)* for Yamaha PianoSoft. Biegel recorded the world premiere of Lalo Schifrin's *Piano Concerto No. 2 - The Americas* with the Bayerischer Rundfunk (Munich Radio Orchestra) for the motion picture soundtrack *Something to Believe In*.

Jeffrey Biegel was the unanimous recipient of the First Grand Prize in the Marguerite Long International Piano Competition and First Prize in the William Kapell/University of Maryland International Piano Competition. He studied at the Juilliard School with Adele Marcus. Biegel teaches at the Conservatory of Music at Brooklyn College and the Graduate Center of the City University of New York.